Also by Judy Rose
Fridge Over Troubled Water

Charlotte Murphy

Judy Rose lives in the Cotswolds with one husband, two sons and seventy llamas. Her inspiration for verse arrived quite suddenly, when a period of enforced bed rest gave her a surprising new angle on the joys of motherhood, domestic bliss and the pursuit of the body beautiful.

JUDY ROSE

MUMMY SAID THE 'B' WORD

HEADLINE

For Paul, with my love

(and with thanks to Olly and Xandi for the title!)

First published in 1997
by HEADLINE BOOK PUBLISHING

1 3 5 7 9 10 8 6 4 2

British Library Cataloguing in Publication Data

Rose, Judy
    Mummy said the 'b' word and other
    poems from the domestic front
    1.English poetry - 20th century
    I.Title
    821.9′14

    ISBN 0 7472 2042 5

Typeset by Letterpart Limited, Reigate, Surrey
Printed and bound in Great Britain by
Mackays of Chatham plc, Chatham, Kent

HEADLINE BOOK PUBLISHING
A division of Hodder Headline PLC
338 Euston Road
London NW1 3BH

Contents

FAMILY MATTERS

Travel Bugbear

A long car journey with my boys,
And, frankly, all's not well,
Yes here we go again, I fear;
Another trip from hell!

For now a violent fight erupts
Pulled hair, bloodcurdling screams,
Oh how I long for in-car calm
JUST ONCE? Huh! In my dreams!

Attempts to keep the peace just make
My steering so erratic.
I cannot referee this lot
In heavy rush-hour traffic.

No hope of concentrating
Or observing highway code.
IN FACT IT IS A MIRACLE
THAT WE STAY ON THE ROAD!

And now we've reached a sudden halt –
They've really gone too far!
That's it! We three ain't going
Any further in this car!

For on this point I'm very clear:
There will be no demurring,
I simply cannot drive this car
While FRATRICIDE'S occurring!

It's His Party . . . And I'll Cry If I Want To!

The big day has arrived at last,
The party has begun.
With twenty darling six year olds
We're in for lots of fun!

For some the party atmosphere
Is proving too exciting;
For half the kids are howling
And those that aren't, are fighting!

High time for Pass the Parcel
Well, this should be a snip;
(Though some are most reluctant
To yield parcel from their grip!)

Now Sophie's inconsolable
She didn't win the prize.
(Her mum's competitive as hell . . .
It comes as no surprise!)

I make some games suggestions, but
'WE CAN'T STAND BLIND MAN'S BUFF!'
(Though only fifteen minutes in . . .
The going's getting tough!)

Inspired I cry, 'It's time for tea!'
Yes, food will be my saviour.
(The poor mites are all starving –
This explains their foul behaviour.)

But so much for the party fayre:
They're very hard to please.
'Why don't you have a sandwich?'
''COS I HATE EGG, JAM AND CHEESE!'

They only eat the Twiglets,
'You rotten lot,' I mutter.
(For this I spent two hours
With the dinosaur-shape cutter!)

Now in the corner of the room
Disaster looms. I swoop . . .
But sadly just too late to catch
That errant ice-cream scoop.

Rice Krispie cakes crushed into rugs
And sofas moist with jelly,
And not-so-yummy sausages
Shoved down behind the telly.

Months later, I still come across
A wayward Hula Hoop
(And other 'nasty finds' such as
What's now Jurassic puke!)

Next year when party time comes round
I'll be there . . . *on condition*
We hire a hall, a referee,
A caterer and . . .
Magician!

Toy Story

Who would have thought that children's toys
Could cause such untold stress?
And I'm not talking cost here —
Nor even endless mess.
My thoughts on this necessitate
A two-fold explanation.
For firstly I mean DANGER
And secondly, FRUSTRATION.

Who would have thought a simple toy
In play, used harmlessly,
Could pose a threat to life and limb
And to one's sanity?
Yes, home feels like a minefield.
I never know for sure
When next my foot will be impaled
On a plastic dinosaur.
When sinking into sofas
Who knows what I may land on?
And days are rare indeed that I
Don't have a Lego to stand on.

That 'Puppy in the Pocket'
May be cute, but — count upon it,
It really loses all its charm
Once you have sat down on it.
It may not give you rabies
But please, take it from me,
This does not mean you won't require
A trip to Casualty!

Those toys! They lie in wait in shoes,
On chairs or in your bed;
Sometimes I cannot see the fun
In toys, it must be said.

And now the second problem
That makes me lose my wits,
And frankly it's par for the course . . .
I mean THE MISSING BITS.
Anticipation's running high:
We'll play the new board game.
But with no dice I have to say
It's never *quite* the same.
The train set would be such great fun,
Had we not lost some track.
And but for three small pieces
The puzzle is intact.

And this mechanical-type crane
Would thrill us all, no doubt
Except for one small detail;
The battery's dropped out.
The farmyard scene is looking bare
And lacks some vital factor;
In short there are no animals,
No farmer and no tractor.
This model kit is claimed to be
The king of such constructions.
Alas, we'll never know for sure –
We can't find the instructions.

I don't begrudge the children toys
But there's no point pretending . . .
Toy Stories in *this* household
Rarely have a happy ending!

Nappy Talk

The brochure's crammed with holidays
Luxurious, exotic,
But vital info's missing
And is making me neurotic.

Priorities have changed round here,
What matters most to me
Is . . . can I purchase nappies there
Of a decent quality?

Who cares about jacuzzis,
The en-suite or sea view?
I want to know we're leakproof
When Baby does a poo!

The local culture? Keep it.
The night life? Can't care less!
I only wish to tread a path
To Inner Nappiness.

What mattered once was 'haute cuisine'
But that's long since forgotten.
What matters now? REFASTENING TABS!
Plus smooth, dry, rash-free bottom.

No matter how that sun beats down
The outlook will be bleak
Unless I have three dozen
To see me through each week.

These days it doesn't take that much
To make this mother happy;
My hopes for our next holiday
Are all pinned on . . .
A nappy!

The Way We Were

I remember my last complete sentence,
It was June '89, half-past ten.
Those words clearly spoken?
'My waters have broken!'
Speech would not be coherent again.

Was it hormones that made my mind fuddled?
Or perhaps lack of sleep? Well, search me.
But those old heady days
Of the well-rounded phrase
Are now just a vague memory.

There are times when I get the impression
That a tentative thought has begun.
But with brain at a loss,
How to put it across?
It retreats to whence it has come.

Though I used to devour the newspapers
And I'd always enjoyed a good read,
Soon all I could do
Was work blearily through
The instructions on Babe's powdered feed.

It seems babies do get to the mothers
In a way they don't get to the dads.
While he talked world affairs
My immediate cares
Were comparing new brands of breast pads.

But the joys of the mother are endless
Though a loss of brain power's incurred,
And the old intellect
Well, deep down I suspect
Is um . . .
Thingy . . .
You know . . .
What's the word?

Dressed To Spill

A few tips for the first-time mum,
There's great joy, heaven knows,
But some adjustments must be made
When it comes to clothes.

Though once you were quite elegant
Dressed with care and style,
Believe me, standards start to plunge
And stay there for some while.

It's goodbye to those power suits,
It's breast not shoulder pad,
And your vital accessory?
A well-stocked changing bag!

It's also time to say goodbye
To linen and to silk.
Hello to fabrics that hold their own
With regurgitated milk.

How to protect one's clothing,
Is something of a riddle;
No matter what, you'll be adorned
By Babe's own-label dribble.

Whenever Baby does a burp
One fact you'll have to face,
No matter where that muslin is
IT WON'T BE THE RIGHT PLACE.

So please do take this sound advice
And try to fill that closet
Exclusively with garments
That will tone just right with posset!

Mummy Said The 'B' Word

'Oooh, Mum,
You said the "B" word!
I heard you, Mum, just now.
You called the lady in that car
A bloody selfish cow!'

'It's okay, Mum,
Don't worry.
I promise — won't tell Dad.
We all know swearing's wicked
And the "B" word's very bad!'

'Hey, Dad,
Mum said the "B" word,
A lady took her space,
She said it very loudly
Went bright red in the face.
And then she told the husband
He had a bloody nerve.
You see, she said it twice, Dad —
And what's an effing perve?'

I Lost My Man To The Internet
(Oh, What A
Tangled Web . . .)

Computer mags in bed were bad enough
A penchant I had good cause to regret,
Alas, these days the going's much more tough
What with his passion for the Internet.
Yes, now he's wont to surf the Superhighway
An indoor sport that takes up all his time.
I'd make it out of bounds, if I had my way
Then maybe I'd get back that man of mine.
A source of information there's no doubt,
New sites to visit, pages to download,
Communing with the world . . . but what about
Her Indoors in the marital abode?
Yes, pity the Web Widow, O wretched female!
Obliged to reach her spouse via his e-mail.

In Praise Of Cats Versus Men or Paws For Thought

How can we count the virtues
Of a fluffy feline friend?
The soft, serene companionship
On which we can depend.
How can we count the many ways
In which they bring us joy?
How rare the moments when
They aggravate us and annoy.

The thing about a cat is that
It never disagrees,
It never criticises
Or says things that will displease.
And one thing you can count upon
Your cat will never mention,
That you have put on lots of weight
Or have pre-menstrual tension.
And when it comes to meal-times,
It's unlikely to complain,
Admit it – have you heard it say:
'Not beef Whiskas again!'

Your cat won't hog the duvet
Snore, or crowd you out of bed.
Your cat will purr and nestle
Sweetly by your side instead.

And in your TV choices
You're unanimous, hurray!
It won't be Kitty who insists
You watch *Match of the Day*.
A cat's presence is relaxing,
Can help relieve your tension
And their demands are very few
Unlike *some* we could mention . . .

There's much to be said for feline friends,
A bond that's hassle free,
Not always how we might describe
The state of matrimony.
But in their favour I must say
I know not male nor spouse
Who has ever left on the kitchen floor
. . . Regurgitated mouse!

Him Outdoors

My husband found a hobby,
A passion you might say,
It took a hold quite gradually
As often is the way.

There weren't that many warning signs
But then, it was my failure
Not to spot the 'giveaway' –
The arrival of a trailer.

For trailers are for animals
This much I understand.
A hasty glance around confirmed;
No creatures on our land.

But I did not express unease
Nor asked the question, 'Why?'
Just sensed that something was ahoof
And heaved a 'What next?' sigh.

Then spouse and trailer left one day
For an unknown destination.
I languished in that twilight zone
'Twixt fear and trepidation.

The minutes and the hours passed by,
Then husband reappeared.
But not alone, I have to say.
(It was just as I'd feared.)

Said gleeful spouse, 'Just wait and see
What I have got for you.
It's gentle, soft and fluffy
From high up in Peru.'

'Paddington Bear', I guessed aloud,
And joked facetiously.
He shook his head. I wondered
What lay in store for me.

And then I saw the llama
Doe-eyed and soft and white
So graceful and so elegant
A most amazing sight.

And this is how it all began
His llama husbandry.
(Of course he could not stop at one –
The rest is history.)

My loved one found a hobby
And llamas charm our life
Now he's a llama farmer –
And I'm a llama farmer's wife!

Some 'hobby'! Nature being what it is, babies abound
and 'Him Outdoors' now has a breeding herd of more
than seventy llamas! Llamas are used for fibre, trekking,
sheep guarding . . . or as pets.

Old King Coal

A sunny Sunday in July
Can only mean one thing:
A rare appearance is in store
Of Barbecuing King.

'I'm in the mood to cook,' says he,
'Let's barbecue today!'
Since this mood strikes but once a year
I don't stand in his way.

But cook's a euphemism
For 'pose by barbecue'
While others busily prepare
The props for You Know Who.

He won't budge from the heating coals
For that's where he belongs,
To poke the fire from time to time
And fiddle with his tongs.

At last the food is ready
The chef is duly cheered.
(Though two words quickly spring to mind
One's 'burnt', the other's 'seared'.)

How Barbecuing King is praised
But frankly, I don't get it!
I did the endless groundwork
And he gets all the credit.

And there he stands, so cool and calm
Which isn't that surprising.
He didn't do the shopping
Nor all that tenderising.

He did not thread all those kebabs
Nor skin those chicken thighs,
Nor season all that mince and get
Sore onion-peeling eyes.

Nor did he make the salads,
Or mix the vinaigrette.
He simply wore the pinny
And lit the odd briquette.

In short he slung some bits of meat
Upon a grilling rack
And did impersonations
Of a pyromaniac.

But maybe I'm ungracious.
Give credit to the fella
For only *half* the guests came down
With chronic salmonella!

Postscript to Old King Coal

I'm going to tell it like it is
Though truth can be a bummer;
One swallow of a charred pork chop
Does not, friend, make a summer!

THESE THINGS WERE
SENT TO TRY US

The Law Of Sod

The things that rile and rattle me . . .
The sardine tin that has no key,
The loo roll that has no beginning,
The lottery I keep not winning,
The size twelve that comes nowhere near,
The clingfilm that will not adhere,
Cold butter that makes holes in bread,
The dead mouse left by cat in bed,
The pen that's never by the phone,
The shopping list that's left at home,
The nonstick pan that always sticks,
The cake mixture that will not mix,
The parking space that's not my size
(That dent in car you can't disguise),
Those wretched cartons that pretend
That they will open other end,
All supermodels everywhere,
The flick-ups I get in my hair,
The eggshell that falls in the whites,
The ladder in the brand new tights,
The Big Mistake bought at the sales,
All sexist, patronising males,
All women who have muscle tone
And miseries who love to
Moan.

Close Encounters Of The Car Kind

I'm sure I'll get into that space
I'll nip in, in reverse
But then recall
It's Husband's car
And long . . . and *new*.
Lips purse.

Just cannot get the angle right
Am sticking out a mile
I notice male observer
Wearing
'Woman parker' smile.

I've broken out into a sweat
While steering tearfully
That lethal combination of
Tight space
And PMT.

At tenth attempt I lose my cool
Slam foot down on the clutch
Select wrong gear
Lurch forward . . . oops!
A tiny bit too much.

That crunching sound forewarns me
Of the horrors I may find.
I urgently reverse . . .
Into the vehicle
Behind.

I should have picked a bigger space
This might have been prevented.
Crowd gathers
Wish 'twas just my pride
That had been badly dented.

Leave details on both windscreens,
Fear much worse when I get back
To face the music,
Husband,
And no doubt
Two-prang attack!

Is This A Digger Which I See Before Me?

(With apologies to William Shakespeare)

Is this a digger which I see before me?
Roadworks again. When will it ever end?
Those temporary lights, familiar story
Of rush-hour jams that drive us round the bend.

I feel the signs of stress, of deep frustration.
I look again; if only it could be
A digger of the mind, a false creation,
But sadly it's the real thing that I see.

It's humid and my blood pressure is rising,
The light goes green, AND THEN GOES RED AGAIN!
And now there are strong words – hardly
   surprising –
Proceeding from this heat-oppressèd brain.

I cannot blame the workmen for such trouble,
They're only players on this messy stage,
But as I feel the pace of my heart double
Oh, how I long to vent my roadwork rage.

Turning Another Cheek

Whatever happened to the single kiss?
One friendly peck to say goodbye, hello.
These days the kissing lark is hit or miss;
You could get done three times! You never know.
This practice hails from continental nations
But has not crossed the Channel easily.
Oh, simple kiss! Now fraught with complications,
As we attempt to guess one, two or three.
I treat excessive kissing with derision
For quality not quantity's the point,
And worse; the hazard of mid-kiss collision
Has left some noses badly out of joint.
Yes – dangerous, pretentious and confusing;
No to the Euro-kiss and facial bruising.

In-Store Detection

On routine expedition
To local superstore
Observe with consternation
Things aren't quite as before.

Yes, once I glided down these aisles
With confidence and ease
Safe in the knowledge I knew where
I'd find the frozen peas.

But now I'm not so shelf-assured
For frankly all's not well;
The staff have rearranged the shop
(To spite the clientèle).

Yes I, once carefree customer,
Engaged in weekly chore,
And now a stressed-out shopper
With a big surprise in-store.

For now I'm in a foreign land
Familiar landmarks gone.
I glance around, note others
Looking shelf-shocked, pale and wan.

I can't locate the sausages
And note hysterically
That there are piles of nappies
Where the yoghurts used to be.

Who could have guessed I'd long for
Just a sighting of baked beans,
Or dread that I might never find
The fig-rolls or crunch creams.

No warnings of this chaos!
A management disgrace
(The check-out tills, of course, we find
Left in their normal place).

A nightmarish scenario
And in it I detect
The work of a misogynist
With little shelf-respect.

I want to vent my rage, my wrath,
Find someone to berate;
The brain behind this plot must be
Well past its 'best by' date.

Yes, just give me five minutes with
The fool behind this folly
Who helped this happy shopper go
Completely off her trolley.

You Know The Drill

The Dentist's chair . . .
Why does it fill us
With such fear and dread?
We brace ourselves
For the ordeal
Each time with hearts of lead.
Why do we break
Into a sweat —
Get knotted up inside
On hearing words
That chill the bones:
'Now, please just open wide.'
Perhaps it is
Because we know
He'll probe each crack, each hole
(And you're the leader
Of the Plaque
Who's blown tartar control).
And then he'll find
That tender nerve . . .
'How does that feel?' he'll ask.
With all his bits
Between your teeth
Replying's quite a task.
But who needs speech
At times like this?
Your loud screams say it all;
He nods. 'I think we'll fill that now.'
'I DON'T AGREE,' you bawl.

And finally
His ticking off
Will really leave you blushing;
'I fear you score
Nil on the floss
And must improve your brushing.'
Gums numb
And most down in the mouth
Your Molar energy depleted,
You thank your stars
That it's six months
Till this hell is repeated.

Never Can Say Goodbye

The attic has reached bursting point
And can't take any more
There's twenty years of piled up things
Now spilling through the door.
The shelves strain under objects that
'Just can't be thrown away'.
And boxes brim with 'useful things
We're bound to need one day'.
Drawers overflow with endless junk
(Saved for posterity),
Plus things in 'why the hell did we
Keep that?'-type category.

But now it's time to sort it out
A task that's monumental.
No room here for nostalgia
Or feeling sentimental.
A ruthless attitude's required
A rigorous attack
With gritted teeth and great resolve
Hold out the first black sack!
Determinedly, I seize a coat
(With wildlife living in it),
And feeling very smug
And strong, I purposefully bin it.

And in this vein, I carry on
For half an hour or so.
From time to time heard muttering,
'Oh yes, *this* has to go.'

And so I happily discard
The mildewed and the musty
The 'decades past its peak of chic',
The broken and the rusty.
And now there is no stopping me
I fill sack after sack
(There's nothing to this sorting lark . . .
Soon have my attic back).

But maybe I've been hasty
Re ease of task at hand.
For soon nostalgia hits me
And things don't go as planned;
The sight of all the baby toys
Has made me misty-eyed,
I try on once-prized garments,
Bell-bottomed and tie-dyed.
I read the bundled letters
I sigh, I cry, I laugh.
I go through *all* the school reports
And *every* photograph.

The hours pass by unnoticed
As I rummage through my past
But when you're sorting memories
You can't go very fast.

Much later, black sacks piled in road
It hits me in a flash;
I can't just chuck my life away!
I've been extremely rash.
To part with my own history
Would be a crime, a sin:
When no one's looking I'll nip out
And bring the lot back in!

One Week In Four

There's a blight that affects many women
It's a syndrome that's hard to ignore;
Transforms angels to bitches
Good mothers to witches
And it comes around one week in four.

You had better watch out, all you partners,
Though it's you she does love and adore;
Things go quickly off-course,
She'll find grounds for divorce
Till things go back to normal once more.

She might burst into tears for no reason
Her reaction out of all proportion;
When emotions run rife
There'll be trouble and strife
So beware – and approach her with caution.

She might fly off the handle for nothing
And a violent act might ensue.
Angry words will be spoken
Precious ornaments broken
And the baddie will always be YOU!

Yes, your world may well end up in turmoil
And your loved one may seem like a stranger
But I strongly advise
That you *don't* criticise
If you do . . . your life may be in danger.

This complete transformation will pain her
She'll despise herself deep in her soul
But this state she bemoans
Is all down to hormones
And is sadly beyond her control.

Make allowances for her condition
Show her kindness and patience galore
Just remember that she
Has got bad PMT –
And it's only for one week in four.

Erroneous Zones

Well – so what if we're more super-wobble than model
And our stomachs aren't flat, or thighs smooth?
So what if we're pear-shaped, or vertically challenged
And all have a few pounds to lose?

And so what if we spot the odd line, flaw or wrinkle
Staring back at us from our reflection?
Just tell me, why should we attempt to live up
To some media myth of perfection?

And who cares if we can't make loose covers or curtains
Or knock up a delicious soufflé?
You're no less of a woman if you don't embroider
Or bake your own bread every day.

If you can't make things seen on *Blue Peter*
And your playdough goes wrong every time,
And you shout at your children and moan at your man,
You're human – it's not such a crime.

Yet at times we are so very harsh to ourselves
Feeling guilt and inadequacy,
Trying hard to live up to an image we have
Of the way 'perfect woman' should be.

Well, it's time we rejected impossible goals
To be thin Superwoman-type clones . . .
We are all doing fine
So let's simply accept
That we all have erroneous zones.

Spring

Buds on the trees
Warmth in the breeze
To birdsong
I awaken.
I thought this might
Inspire a poem
But I was quite
Mistaken.

Summertime Blues

There's nothing like
This woman's wrath.
It would make
A grown man cower,
When tuning in
To Radio Four
I find Cricket
Not *Woman's Hour*!

Thank You

I'd like to write a thank-you rhyme
For a really lovely night
But I'm having awful problems
And just can't get it right.
It's not that I am lost for words
Or that my brain is tired,
Or that an evening spent with you
Does not leave me inspired . . .
I hope that you won't take offence
Or think me quite perverse . . .
It's just the evening does not seem
To lend itself to verse!

I'd rave about the hors d'oeuvres
But I'm such an awful speller
So cannot praise your gwackermowl
Nor mention mottzereller.
The casserole was super
And the veg were quite divine
(So I grant you I have something
That would constitute one line).
Well, pud left me a final chance
Before the meal was over
But I couldn't find a thing to rhyme
With *strawberry pavlova*.

Of course there was the company,
Quite charming but I fear
I couldn't get a word of sense
From the Russian engineer.

The chiropodist was chatty
And she really knows her stuff,
But one hour on verrucas . . .
I had more than heard enough!
The woman with the waist-length curls
I feel deserves a mention
In what would be the world's first verse
About a hair extension.

Yes, the evening was a great success
I had a brilliant time
Though sadly quite unable
To express my thanks in rhyme.
Next time I come for dinner
Your humble friend suggests
Please let me choose the menu
And also vet the guests.

KEEPING UP
APPEARANCES

Thoughts On The Thigh

There was a time when shafts of light
Fell softly 'twixt these thighs;
Once slim and firm, but o'er the years
I've witnessed their demise.
Once quite restrained but now I sense
They have a separate will;
They seem to go on wobbling
Long after I've stood still!
Once unobtrusive, merely 'there'
But nowadays it seems
They are a true impediment
When pulling on my jeans.
You say 'Work out and diet?'
But such options I decry . . .
I'll just accept that it's my fate
To heave a heavy thigh!

Admitting Defeat

No one could say I haven't tried,
Give credit where it's due
But when it comes to diets
I've done all I can do.

I've had it with the Cambridge,
The F Plan and the Y,
The gruelling flat stomach plan
And Ms Conley's 'hip and thigh'.

Despite untold upheaval
I tried food combination;
I'd say I went the way of Hay
With high anticipation.

The low fat and the high starch,
The carbohydrate buster –
I've followed every one with all
The verve that I could muster.

I've read my Callan Pinkney,
Devoured my Audrey Eaton
But reader, I must tell you that
I'm well and truly beaten.

The acid test is . . . the results,
One fact I can't ignore;
Post diet, there is *more* of me
Than what there was before!

The experts always tell us
That diets make you fat.
'Give up! It will not work!' they say.
I'll have to second that.

You may not end up skinny
But what you can't deny . . .
You save £££s on the diet books
You simply do not buy!

Absolutely Flabless

At last! The hottest new technique
For effective fat reduction
Can be performed in your own home,
They call it 'Flab-O-Suction'.

The Flab-O-Suction kit is at
A hardware store near you,
And once you get it home
You'll be amazed what it can do!

The system's set up in a jiff,
Involves one quick manoeuvre.
You simply take the nozzle
And attach it to your Hoover.

You place the nozzle on your flab,
Then switch the power on,
You'll hear a flab-o-sucking sound . . .
Hey presto! That flab's gone!

In truth, reactions have been mixed
To this product, so new-fangled;
Some have been quite delighted.
Others left completely mangled.

The Bottom Line

Oh gravity. Oh passing years
One simply can't ignore.
You leave parts of the body
Quite unlike they were before.
Of course there's lots of help at hand
For the sadly drooping breast.
(You'll know if you've got one of these
By doing the pencil test!)
Yes, with assistance from your bra
Some pertness is recouped.
But where is the support the day
You find your bottom's drooped?

Of course, you could try counselling
Or join a self-help group.
But frankly this will not do much
For chronic bottom droop.
You might try buttock clenching
Liposuction's somewhat quicker,
But more uplifting's got to be
Underwiring of the knicker.
Yes, when that tired posterior
Requires a pick-me-up
You'll nip down to the undie shop
And choose your buttock-cup!

Yes! Gravity *will* be defied,
And it's my firm belief
We'll put the droop behind us
With a well-wired Wonder-Brief.

Bare-Faced Truth

If I am ever bold enough
To venture out of doors
Without a dab of blusher
To perk up my pallid pores,
I always get the same response –
Concern and sympathy,
'Are you all right? You look so pale!
You don't look well to me!'

And when in gay abandoned mood
I cry, 'Oh what the hell!'
And leave off the mascara
And go *'au naturel'*,
I know that someone will remark
As they are wont to do;
'You're run down, dear. I think you need
An early night, or two.'

To face the world without some 'help'
In my case takes some valour,
While pale and interesting suits some
On me it's deathly pallor.
The deep concern aroused suggests
That 'as Nature intended'
Is great in theory,
But for me
Not to be recommended.

I deepen blush, I lengthen lash
It works and I can tell
When people stop and say to me,
'You're really looking well.'
Cosmetically dependent,
A sad and poignant tale,
But it's preferable
To sympathy
And a whiter shade of pale.

Bad Hair Day

Just when you want to look your best
It always is the way,
One look at mess on head confirms
You're having a bad hair day.

You know the score: BIG interview
THE party, THAT hot date.
Despite threats and cajoling
Hair won't co-operate.

Things do not always go as planned
That old familiar story;
Read 'just been pulled through hedge' look
For well-groomed crowning glory.

Flick-ups at forty are not cute
A fact one cannot hide
(It's little consolation
That they're only on one side).

My fringe looks like it's just been 'nuked'
A source of deep regret;
Too bad the 'mad professor' look
Has not quite caught on yet.

In vain I try to recreate
That sleek look that I crave,
No matter how I mousse and gel
That hair just won't behave.

And products that all promised
To tame the wildest tress
Do not de-fuzz, de-curl, de-frizz
But boy – do they depress!

So much for all my efforts
To add body and condition;
I curse the hair I've grown to hate
In this war of attrition.

There's only so much one can do
So that, I fear, is that!
Just two solutions spring to mind –
Stay in
Or wear
A hat!

Hair Today . . . Groan Tomorrow

She pours hot wax upon my legs
And spreads it all around.
The air fills with my plaintive cries
And a nasty ripping sound.

For I have chosen torture
In the serious pursuit
Of beautifying legs that have
Got seriously hirsute.

I could use cream, or I could shave
But opt for agony
To have legs that are silky smooth
And follically free.

Some will not understand this choice
But it would be simplistic,
To simply write me off as one
Who's mad or masochistic.

The thing is, once you've done the deed
And recovered from the pain
For six whole weeks those legs
Will not need pruning back again.

And now . . . what of my torturer?
We really get on fine;
She gives me hell, I glare at her,
She waxes and I whine.

She's quite immune to my distress
And pleas loud and frenetic
That rend the air between each rip;
'I NEED AN ANAESTHETIC!'

She carries on her cruel craft
Devoid of sympathy,
As, singing softly to herself,
She waxes, lyrically.

FOOD FOR THOUGHT

Egg-White Blues

While browsing round my fridge
I'm assailed
By guilty pangs
That bowl of languid egg-whites pleads
'Make us into meringues.
Use us for Baked Alaska
Or a lovely light pavlova,
But please do not leave us unwhipped
Left idle and left over.'

Slam fridge door shut!
That's all I need
A silent whites reproach.
Beginning to have deep regrets
At having used those yolks.
But I'm not in a whipping mood
Though all too well aware
That all that's needed is a bowl,
A whisk, and lots of air.

No need for any action now
They'll last a few more weeks
Until I get that sudden urge
To beat them into peaks.
For now, I'll push them to the back
So I won't be harangued
By the poignant sight
Of sad egg-whites
Unfulfilled and unmeringued.

Ode To Delia Smith

(To be hummed along to the tune of 'Summertime')

Summertime
And the cooking is easy.
That is if . . .
You've got Delia's book.
Food tastes great
And it's fabulous-looking,
With the help of this woman
You'll soon be an excellent cook.

Wintertime
And the cooking is easy.
That is if . . .
You've consulted our Dele.
Christmas fayre
Has been given new meaning,
It's goodbye to dry turkey
Hello to the next gourmet meal.

One of these days
I will write her a letter.
In it I'll tell her
Just how grateful I am.
Nowadays
All my cooking is easy,
And believe me
If I can be Delia'd
Then anyone can!

Going For Grilled

I never fry my food these days
I 'Go for Grilled' instead
It's healthier
It makes more sense –
Unless we're talking 'egg.'

Eggs slide right through that grill pan
In the twinkling of an eye,
You've got no choice;
Whip out that fat
And give that egg a fry.

And then there's chips and onions –
Both exceptions to my rule.
To shove them
Underneath a grill
You'd have to be a fool.

And stir-fried veg, hash brown, popcorn
With the best-intentioned will
Cannot be plucked
From frying pan
And popped under a grill.

My 'Go for Grilled' philosophy
Perhaps needs qualifying;
I always grill
My food these days . . .
Except when it needs frying!

And So To Bread

Has anybody else observed
The 'new loaf' revolution?
The strangest breads appear these days
In frightening profusion.

Why complicate the matter
With new fads? . . . It's just not right;
I've got enough on my plate
Choosing wholemeal, brown or white.

For some, 'traditional' won't do
It's nowadays deemed smarter
To go for more exotic breads
With strange names like Ciabatta.

Call me old-fashioned if you like,
But such trends I denounce.
I will not purchase bread whose name
I can't even pronounce.

In days gone by, the granary
Or cottage loaf sufficed
A wholemeal or a nice white tin,
Large, small, uncut or sliced.

Yes, in those days you'd buy a loaf
And you would simply know
That it was made without a doubt
From normal bread-type dough.

But now there is no telling,
And I have been nonplussed
To find sun-dried tomatoes
Lurking underneath that crust.

And when I spied the walnut bread
I thought, 'There's some mistake –
A mix-up at the bakery.
These should be in a CAKE!'

And what to make of olive bread?
The fact we have to face
Is frankly, in the good old days
An olive knew its place.

Yes, when it comes to choosing loaves
I draw the old bread-line,
While others charter newer ground
A large tin suits me fine.

This penchant for the new, I feel,
Has grown out of proportion.
And my advice is simple:
Approach these loaves with caution!

Help From An Unexpected Sauce

Are your chicken breasts boring and bland?
Well, I've been there and quite understand.
But you'll soon say goodbye
To the tasteless and dry
For considerable help is at hand.

If your culinary skills are quite poor
And you find scanning cookbooks a bore,
Just admit you've been beat,
And get out there and cheat
For my dears, there are short cuts galore.

You'll find sauces in jars, cans and bottles
From the subtle to those with more 'throttle'.
Thai, Mexican, Cajun,
Szechuan, French, Malaysian,
And good value, they don't cost a lot(tle).

The groundwork is done in a trice,
Take your chicken and joint, strip or dice,
And for perfect digestion
There's a serving suggestion
And it normally goes 'Serve with rice'.

So dull *pollo* – *finito!* No more!
Check out sauce shelves in your superstore,
You'll soon find that your chicken
Will be finger-lickingly
Good . . . as like never before.

Next time, menu-wise, you get stuck
Seize that sauce. Clasp that can. Try your luck.
Whet the old appetite
With some chicken tonight
And you'll soon have them all going 'Cluck'.

Spreading The Word

Could someone please assist me here
And shed a little light
On what to spread on bread these days;
Is there a wrong or right?
Just when you think you've got it straight
A new decree is uttered;
It's either, 'Switch to Low-Fat Spreads!'
Or else, 'Bread should be buttered!'

One minute low-fat spreads are 'In'
If they're unsaturated
(And butter's off the menu
All benefits negated!)
Next minute butter's not so bad
Consumed in moderation,
And doubt is cast upon those spreads
Held dear by half the nation.

Well butter seems a healthy choice;
I've seen ads on TV
Where grass is green and fresh and pure
And cows graze rustically,
But low-fat spreads are better
For waistline and for heart,
And taste so much like butter
You can't tell them apart.

Consumers need to know the truth
And must not be denied!
We want to have this matter –
Marge or butter – clarified.
'Eat butter, rich and natural.'
'Eat margarine . . . stay fitter.'
The battle of the spreads goes on.
I can't believe it's not bitter!

Let Us Now Praise Famous Spreads Again

Some seek adventure in their food,
Rate cuisine from afar,
But with a Marmite finger
You know just where you are.

MATTERS OF THE

HEART

Time Bomb

The magic hour of eight has long since passed
I've watched the minutes slowly turn to hours
He's late again . . . that's it . . . the die is cast!
He's had it (even if he does bring flowers)!
'I lost all track of time' his weak excuse
(I'll kill him if he tries that one again).
'You've got a watch,' I scream. 'You're not obtuse,
Well, look at it! The little hand's on TEN!'
Unpunctual fool. I'll stand for this no more.
I just can't play this waiting game for ever.
You've blown it, Sunshine. Farewell, *mon amour*,
For I don't hold with 'better late than never'.
This love of ours might well have been sublime.
If only, dear heart . . . you could be on time.

A Fine Romance

What joy, we'll soon be married
You'll be my lifelong mate,
But first of all, my darling,
Let's get a few things straight.

In order that we can achieve
Domestic harmony,
There are a few small matters
On which we should agree.

Of course it stands to reason
We'll share the household chores,
Except for ironing your shirts . . .
That job, my sweet, is yours!

Our lives will soon be intertwined
Oh, roll on happy day!
But first you'll have to promise me
That you'll bath every day.

And though I love you as you are,
You've got some weight to lose;
You'll have to give up junk food
And cut down on the booze.

I know this might seem awfully harsh
But feel that you should know
I can't stand stale tobacco –
Your pipe will have to go.

And knowing that I can't stand sport
I'm sure you'll understand
That football's out on Saturday
And Test Matches are banned.

When I think of our future
My heart feels fit to burst
But just a few more details
Need clarifying first.

Yes, one more thing, my darling,
Before you can be mine.
This prenuptial agreement . . .
Just read it through
AND SIGN!

Nine O'Clock Ooohs

I've got a deep affection for
That newsman,
Michael Buerk.
But given the odd hours he keeps
I doubt if it
Would wuerk.

Brazen Valentine

Violets are purple
Roses are pink
I'll say no more, handsome,
Than
Nudge, Nudge,
Wink, Wink!

Dual-Purpose Valentine

When I'm apart from you, my love,
The minutes seem like hours.
PS: On your way home tonight,
Please don't forget the flowers.
I cherish and adore you,
And more words of that ilk
And NB – re the lingerie,
I only wear pure silk.
You are my lover, my best friend,
My idol and my mentor,
And if you're bringing chocolates
Buy Thorntons (fruit cream centre).
You are the man I most admire
You're sensitive and clever,
So no doubt have remembered
That diamonds are for ever.

Ode To A Youthful-Looking Fifty Year Old

Dear friend, on this auspicious day
I send my best to you.
But though you say you're fifty
I can't believe it's true.
Perhaps it's being young at heart
Or is it in your genes?
Or maybe you've invested in
Some 'youth replenish' creams?
So tell me, what's your secret?
For it really does the trick.
Your answer on a postcard please,
And send it to me
Quick!

CLOTHES ENCOUNTERS

Waist Not . . . Want Not

Oh yes, I did once have a waist,
A place to put a belt,
And I would clinch it nice and tight
And look all slim and svelte.

But that was quite some time ago
And now I must divulge
That what once was, has been replaced
By rampant midriff bulge.

And nowadays of course I opt
For clothes that just flow free,
And all those belts that waisted once
Are wasted now on me!

Thongs Ain't What They Used To Be

A leather strip
For reins, or whip
The thong
Once knew its place

But now
Some people wear them
ON THE BEACH
(It's a disgrace!)

Bleak Hose

I shop and find the perfect dress
An off-white silky dream,
With matching shoes and handbag
(Accessories to the cream)
But when at last the big day comes
I'm racked with misery;
One thing has been forgotten –
The toning hosiery!
What passes as 'my lingerie'
Is thoroughly inspected.
I note the tights department
Has been woefully neglected.
There's navy blue and black and grey
Dark shades in great profusion,
All tangled inextricably
In spaghetti-style confusion.
And every single shade of brown
From autumn mist to russet
(Albeit those not laddered
Are impaired around the gusset).
But 'cream' or 'flesh' or 'nearly nude'?
Oh woe! No pair in sight,
Nor anything to complement
My vision in off-white.
OK – I've not much fashion sense
But one thing I *do* know
Is floaty whites and winter tights
Together do not go.

But time is running very short
My options – sadly few.
It looks as though
These tan pop-socks
Will simply have to do!

Ode To A Stylish Friend

Ma chère,
You have got so much style,
You always look so *chic*,
All dressed up in your *haute-couture*
Très élégante, très slick.
So well-groomed from your polished shoes
Right to your well-coiffed hair.
How come you ended up with
So much bloody *savoir-faire*?
Quite simply you have got it,
Got that *'je ne sais pas quoi'*.
Perhaps some will rub off on me?
I doubt it.
Love
From
Moi.

Brief Encounters

Oh, why did I wear this bra today?
In subtle washed-too-often grey,
And frayed in such a fetching way,
A charming sight!

My knickers past their bin-by date
Elastic gone, a common fate,
Far too much strain from excess weight,
Plus laddered tights.

And why was it my fate to share
With pin-thin nymphet over there
In her designer underwear?
It's just not right!

I should have washed my hair, I know,
That extra stone will have to go,
Good grief, my crows' feet really show
In this harsh light!

Oh mirror, mirror on the wall
I don't like what I see at all.
The lure of shopping seems to pall,
I look a fright.

Yet I forge on, try suit and dress,
An optimist at heart, I guess,
These look all wrong, this looks a mess,
That's far too tight.

Let's face it, things have not gone well,
And this, a shopping trip from hell,
Will end in tears, I know full well.
Oh, sorry plight.

I've really had all I can take,
To shop for clothes was a mistake.
I need a coffee . . . and some cake
To put me right.

Two doughnuts and a macaroon
Relieve my spirits, lift my gloom,
Dispel thoughts of hell's changing room,
I thought they might . . .

All's well . . .
Haven't lost my appetite!

Breathe In

The party dress you bought was tight,
Extremely tight! You knew it.
You thought, 'I'll lose those extra pounds
In time,' but sadly blew it.
A voice did say, 'Go up a size!'
But you chose to ignore it.
And now the big day has arrived
There's only one thing for it . . .

Breathe in, BREATHE IN,
And don't let go
Or everyone will know
The true extent
Of tummy
You're trying not to show.

Breathe in, BREATHE IN,
Chest out, head high
And nobody will guess
How difficult
It was to do
The zip up on your dress.

Breathe in, BREATHE IN,
Act naturally
Above all, try to smile.
Although your stomach muscles
Give you pure hell
All the while.

Breathe in, BREATHE IN,
But when you walk

Do try to look at ease
And not as though
You're made of wood
Between the neck and knees.

Breathe in, BREATHE IN,
And do not eat!
However much you're tempted,
For only this
Will guarantee
Disaster is prevented.

Breathe in, BREATHE IN
And do not laugh.
The hazards are quite plain,
You're bound to cause those fragile seams
Irrevocable strain.

Apart from this, enjoy yourself
Try not to think about
The fact that you've
Still got three hours
Before you can
BREATHE OUT.

Fat Accompli

Bikini-clad upon the beach
Observe with some distress
Pre-holiday crash diet
Was not complete success.

Clothes Encounters Of
The Last-Minute Kind

An eleventh-hour drama
Panic rising, tearing hair,
I need help to find 'The Outfit'
(Given lack of fashion flair).
I'm adrift with fabrics, colours,
No clue what will go with what
To achieve a stylish image
(Basic dress sense I ain't got),
I need women kind and helpful
Women who will tell me straight
If the garment I am trying
Shows up all my excess weight.
Women who sense what will flatter
And of course, on top of that,
Who can make my legs look longer
And my bulgy bits look flat.
Women who stay calm and placid
When I shriek, 'It's for tomorrow!'
Who, with lots of fashion know-how,
Ease last-minute shopper's sorrow.

Are you out there somewhere, ladies?
I do need you, heaven knows.
Can you help this fashion victim?
I'd be grateful,
Judy Rose.